TRYING
TO SURPRISE
GOD

for Nell
all best
Peter
FCTE '91

Trying
to
SURPRISE
God

Peter Meinke

[signature: Peter Meinke]

University of Pittsburgh Press

Published by the University of Pittsburgh Press, Pittsburgh, Pa. 15260
Feffer and Simons, Inc., London
Manufactured in the United States of America

Library of Congress Cataloging in Publication Data

Meinke, Peter.
    Trying to surprise God.

    (Pitt poetry series)
    I. Title.
PS3563.E348T78   811'.54   80-54062
ISBN 0-8229-3434-5
ISBN 0-8229-5326-9 (pbk.)

Acknowledgment is made to the following publications, which first published some of the poems in this book: *CCL Newsletter, Cosmopolitan, Crux, The Devil's Millhopper, The Educational Forum, The Florida Review, Ladies' Home Journal, Local Muse 2, Michigan Quarterly Review, Motive, New Orleans Review, The New Republic, The New York Quarterly, The Red Clay Reader, Sports Poems,* and *Yankee.*

"Advice to My Son," "In Gentler Times," "Portrait: White on White," and "The Death of the Pilot Whales" first appeared in *The Antioch Review,* copyright 1965, 1966, 1967, and 1968 by The Antioch Review, Inc., and are reprinted by permission of the editor. "Preacher, Said the General," is reprinted by permission from the March 27, 1968, issue of *The Christian Century,* copyright 1968, Christian Century Foundation. "Elephant Tusks," "The Artist," and "Azaleas" were originally published in the December 1978 issue of *Poetry.*

The author wishes to thank the Florida Council of Fine Arts for a creative writing fellowship, during which some of these poems were written.

The publication of this book is supported by grants from the National Endowment for the Arts in Washington, D.C., a Federal agency, and the Pennsylvania Council on the Arts.

for my Mother and Father

CONTENTS

CONTENTS

TRYING
TO SURPRISE
GOD

SUPERMARKET

My supermarket is bigger than your supermarket. That's
what America's all about. Nowhere am I happier,
nowhere am I more myself. In the supermarket, there
you feel free. Listen: the carts roll
on their oiled wheels, the cash register sings
to the Sound of Music, the bagboys are unbearably polite!
Everywhere there are lies, but in the supermarket we speak truth.
The sallow young man by the cornstarch bumps my cart,
I tell him, There are always two brothers. One is
hardworking, serious. The other is good-looking but worthless;
he drinks, he is a natural athlete, he seduces Priscilla
Warren whom the older brother loves, and then abandons her.
Yes, cries the sallow young man, O my god yes!
Everywhere there are lies, I lie to my classes, I say,
Eat this poem. Eat that poem. *Good* for you.
I say, Sonnets have more vitamins than villanelles,
I give green stamps for the most vivid images.
But in the supermarket truth blows you over like a clearance sale.
I meet Mrs. Pepitone by the frozen fish, dark circles
under her dark eyes. I tell her, If we had met 16 years earlier
in the dairy section perhaps, everything would have been different.
Yes! Mrs. Pepitone cracks a Morton pie in her bare hands, lust
floods the aisles, a tidal wave, everyone staring
at everyone else with total abandon; Mr. Karakis is streaking
through the cold cuts! Outside, the lies continue.
We lie in church, we say
Buy Jesus and you get Mary free. If you have faith
you can eat pork, dollar a chop.
We give plaid stamps for the purest souls.

I meet Sue Morgan by the family-sized maxi-pads. Or
is it mini-pads?—Or is it mopeds? In the supermarket
everything sounds like everything else. I tell her,
You can see azaleas even in the dark, the white ones
glow like the eyes of angels. I tell her, Azaleas
are the soul of the South, you kill all azaleas
Jimmy Carter will shrivel like a truffle. Yes,
she exclaims, Hallelujah! And still the lies
pile up on the sidewalk, they're storming
the automatic doors. Mr. Hanratty the manager throws himself
in front of the electronic beam, he knows this means
he will be sterile forever, but the store comes first:
the lies retreat to the First National Bank
where they meet no resistance. Meanwhile,
in the supermarket I am praising truth-in-advertising
laws, I am trying to figure the exact price per ounce,
the precise percentage of calcium propionate. And
for you, my tenderest darling, to whom I always return
laden with groceries, I bring Spaghetti-O's and chocolate
kisses, I tip whole shelves into my cart, the bag boys
turn pale at my approach, they do isometric exercises.
But I know this excess is unnecessary,
I say, My friends, think Small, use the 8-item line, who
needs more than 8 items? All you really need is
civility, honesty, courage, and 5 loaves of wheatberry bread.
Listen friends, Life is no rip-off, the oranges are full of
juice, their coloring the best we can do, why do you think
we live so long?   So long.

My dear friends, the supermarket is open. Let us begin.

I

Trout

TROUT

Struga Poetry Festival 1979

Look! how the bright green water spills
like dye from the spring to stain the darker
blue of Ohrid Lake. Muscular eels
weave in and out, and the trout flicker

The magic Macedonian trout are under siege,
their eggs devoured by California trout—
larger but less tasty. One thinks,
Capitalist swine! General Motors! CIA!
But no: California trout
were dumped in the lake by the Albanians
who never apologize, never explain. They wear
white skullcaps or black fezzes, weave
in and out of mountains like a secret code.

Grape brandy   peach brandy
juniper and plum
white coffee   Turkish coffee
laced with rum

In the first-class hotel, schools
of force-fed poets flicker and eddy.
Ah, the big poets eat the little poets,
they nibble each other with tentative teeth,
the little ones lurk in the shadow
of a large drink: *Na zdrowie! Skol!*
In the lobby poems pile up like peppers,
dried out but dangerous, get your red hots here!
I bite a fat sestina, terrific!
In my heart, the blood weaves in and out,
it is half-alcohol by now, it whispers drunkenly
in the pool of my ear. *Trout,* it hisses,
remember the trout!

7

In the blue ring of mountains
as the sun climbs
the road weaves in and out
like hidden rhyme

Our driver is clearly insane and happy,
doesn't speak English but occasionally tries.
Fuck Stalin, he says pleasantly, passing
a horse and wagon on a blind curve.
I keep my eyes on the road. I would like
to be an *old* poet some day. Maybe tomorrow.
By the road, fields of faded sunflowers
nod like unread poets in the naked light;
behind them, muezzins mount their holy missiles
pointed at Allah's eye: they, too,
on the hour, chant and cry.

Yaseen   Marit   Rafael   Klaus
Albert   Marianne   Tomasz   Staus

Why is it we always turn toward the small things?
The guide drones on about St. Sofie's Church:
The wide of the walls is seven meters . . .
Magnificent, and yet you turn and say
See the bees in the rose tree, see
that wreath of peppers on the wall! Best of all,
turning a corner, we saw the old poet
standing alone beneath the dark-beamed homes,
blue cap tilted, weathered jacket,
lost, or lost in thought. His words weave in and out
of my mind, starquakes in an inner galaxy
casting its cold and hopeless light
on an ocean of blood.
The California trout *will* eat the Macedonian trout.

8

We start things, and they acquire
an energy of their own
until we are swept away at last and stand,
like the old poet, alone
in the alley of our bones
waiting for the end with fingers crossed,
not exactly lost. I think my life has been spent
under water. May God protect old poets
in their loneliness.

Even here, politics and passion
blossom like a sore
one is called a fascist
one is called a whore
Poetry knows no borders
its country is the soul
but where are the Russians?
the Bulgarians? the Poles?

The trellised arbors, the old tiled rooftops.
The men are dancing in the street!
How is that house still standing?
And the Turks did this and that
in the Seventeenth Century, or was it the Eleventh?
Why can't I remember these centuries?
This mosaic floor was third, I'm almost sure
but just as the guide explained
the disco band below the fortress blared.

I pick a thorn from the rose tree
you pick a rose from the thorn tree
I pick a pear from the plum tree
you pick a plum from the pear tree

9

Among the dancers with linked arms
the old poet weaves in and out. Are you surprised?
he asks. No, I am not, though his poems
have surprised me for years.
Pop-eyed poets prance in a circular fashion,
slivovitz and coffee battle for control.
And when I held hands with Yaseen
I was alarmed
by the warmth of his hands.
The long Indian and the little Indian
make formal gestures; I bow, you curtsy.
I am seeing visions! Ghostly silhouettes
of poets follow them on stage, like
electric auras. But the old poet's is almost
detached from him, a dancing partner,
a pure white mirror image. In our room
our arms weave in and out, they
weave in and out,
and suddenly I know that I am blessed!
We shall make love on the beach Macedonian style!
We shall drink cold white wine and swim to Albania!
We shall write a poem to the old poet and slip it
under his door. Yes. We won't wake him.
We shall slip it under his door.

God bless all poets, small and great
God bless this fading tapestry
and bless the trout in Ohrid Lake
doomed in their darkness, shining, free

10

ROBERT FROST IN WARSAW

When I saw birches in Wasienki Park
leaning against the wind, I thought of you,
old ghost, so strongly have you claimed those trees
for us. Even here, four thousand miles away
from Derry or Franconia, your voice,
through foreign though familiar leaves, whispers
that the human heart can neither forfeit
nor accept responsibilities. Even
here, where storms far wilder, blacker, than those
which strike New Hampshire have torn up the stones
and thrown uncounted populations
into hells we only read about, your poems
proclaim ambiguous affirmation
in the dark. I sit here in a rented room
with you, heart pumping as I read your lines,
and think of parents, wife, and children
who travel with me complicated roads
beneath a winter sky that hides the stars.
They tell me you were selfish: it may be so.
I know you spoke to me through birches in
Wasienki Park, kindly, and brought me home.

A BLESSING

for C. C. and H. D.

To be ill in a foreign country
on a train alone with your language
while the harsh peasant houses
slip by like familiar accusations:

> *Sick because you're impure or weak,*
> *worms gnaw those who refuse to believe,*
> *each wound the body's rush of shame —*

to be ill in a foreign country
as I was saying, therefore,
is the good Lord's blessing:
what can we fear from strangers?
Let me die with no name
on a train to Albania
where even my passport
is invalid—

THE LADIES WHO SHOVEL THE SNOW

The ladies who shovel the snow are dwarves
with large hands. They don't work very hard,
their shovels pieces of plywood
on a witch's broomstick. When they are through
they muscle on the buses with heads down,
unstoppable. When they laugh, children whimper,
small animals cower in corners.
When they smile, the bus caves in.

Where do they come from, these creatures?
They survived the War, they rose from the ashes
of Warsaw, they sit on the buses
holding cut flowers in their broken fingers.
In their eyes the flames still flicker,
the film is preserved; the knock on the door
deafens the mouse in its dark closet.

LETTER FROM WARSAW

for Kathleen McDonald

Copernicus sits on the heart of Europe, lost
in thought, his back to the Academy
on the corner of Nowy Swiat, the New World.
His noble brow is dark, his hand outstretched,
the day itself is dark and cold, the month,
the year the boots the eyes the bones the ashes.
In his left hand he holds the galaxy,
in his right (sometimes) a pigeon, also dark.

The universe is dark, he says, the sun is farther
than we thought.
                    The mind is free.

He swivels his huge head. He looks behind.
You never heard this, he says. Don't quote me.
He shuts his blackened eyes. They open shrewdly
as I pass. Change money? the pigeon cries

Here as everywhere the couples interlock—
more so than Paris, more than Rome, because
the Poles are perfect existentialists,
neither happy nor free. We burn like arrows
from the classic bow, in helpless flight,
or heat-led missiles nosing out the warmest
target, to destroy on contact. The bleak
apartments bloom through smoke,
a futuristic garden where paranoiac
petals blow in the northern wind.
Mother, to what shall we cling? You'd say *Love*
and Music. Both grow here: one trembles
without privacy in crowded buses,
taverns, thin-walled rooms; the other,
an alcohol available to all,

14

spreads its dark pool
to close our eyes and numb the abscessed pain.
Surprised by tears, I listen to my friend
with unpronounceable name playing the Polonaise:
even the chandeliers applaud, flowers
enough to fill a common grave.

What is art but God in the blood
crying to get out into this world?

Mother,
I remember listening to you play Chopin,
the *Marche Funèbre*, Sonata in B Minor—
nothing too difficult or esoteric—
your trembling fingers and panic-stricken eyes
in the dark house in Brooklyn, where Grandpa
and poor paralyzed Uncle George refused
to talk to one another for thirteen years.
Chopin, then, was a lesson to be learned.
He still is. In Warsaw, they played his music
punishable by death, in shadowed rooms
off old Krochmalna Street, long since destroyed.

Art is not democratic, after all,
it is not equal: children
do not write the Polonaise,
their prodigal fingers plunking out
virtuoso combinations without heart.
The static music of computers
blossoms in patches of dry paralysis,
like *Walden II*, or rolfing, or
illustrated manuals of sex:

they soil the air with blooms unholy
and irrelevant. Mother, you wanted beauty
for your children, and fresh air. Where
can we go but to the dignified cathedral
whose soaring arches stretch us beyond ourselves?

The first law is clarity, or should be,
to see, as under a microscope, what is killing us,
the shape of evil, the number of its heads,
the teeth in each head, the sharpness of each tooth.
To taste its brass and filth, to make
the tongue retract, mouth dry up, the throat constrict
till every breath is pain. Clean to the bone.
Then to begin again.

The second law is beauty, or will be,
when our cities are leveled to the ground
and the trees planted. When houses
go up there will be space between them,
high ceilings, and relations between the spaces,
where light and air mingle like music
on our souls. I told you once we had none
and you cried. But you were right:
I feel it here in Warsaw with the strains of Chopin
rising through the fog above the river
that has seen the beating heart of Europe
bleed like a crimson torrent down a slope
till every stone grew slick. And still the music sings.

Ah, mother, you Irish romantic,
you would love the Poles. You burned for beauty
in a world recalcitrant
to poor kids from Brooklyn. You did all your work
and more; your teachers were as ignorant
as the fat pigeons burbling by our door.

Mother, my brave darling,
the third law might have been
Love your mother.
But we have too many laws
so the third law is
There shall be only those two laws.

II

Azaleas

AZALEAS

In the morning, in December
they lean like flares over our brick pathway,
vessels of fragrant energy,
their bright explosions enclosed by the frailest membrane:
they tremble with their holy repressions.
We watch; we tremble, too. We learn.

They thrive on acid, these azaleas; they burn
in darkness, loving the shadows of old oaks
whose broken leaves flutter down to feed
their flowering fantasies.

For surely azaleas are not real, they grow
in some deep wilderness of soul, some known
ideal of vulnerability made palpable,
whose thin petals float dying to the ground
even as we walk by, without touching.
Our very presence seems to kill.

We know more than we can say: we live
in waves of feelings and awareness
where images unfold and grow
along the leafwork of our nerves and veins;
and when one morning late in March
we walk out on our porch and see
the white azaleas open to the air
we recognize them from our dreams
as every cell projects our affirmation.

O Pride of Mobile, Maiden Blush,
Prince of Orange, President Clay:
the names are humorous examples
of human hubris—O Glory of Sunninghill!

And yet they're touching, too: my salmon-
colored Duc de Rohan's fragile aristocracy
doomed like his forebears to lose his head;
your Elegans, that early bloomer,
whose petals lie like butterflies on our walk
or pastel Kleenex thickly strewn
in some orgy of melancholy weeping. . . .

Dwarves and Giants, Pinkshell, Flame—
O my dear, so many azaleas are dying!
We must have a party! Here! This afternoon!

PING-PONG

Outside, the children play ping-pong
beneath the trees. Click-clock click-clock
the ball ticks back & forth through
shadow and leaflight, paddles flash
red and green, red
and green to the eternal
amazement of squirrels in the branches
of field mice in the scattered woodpile

Inside, the halls are ankle deep in blood
the mother hunches in the closet the
father rages through the house breaking mirrors.
Behind the refrigerator the mouse
with broken neck testifies to the reality
of the situation: There is something wrong it
is no one's fault. Roaches drop in saucers
the spider spins with total concentration

This is not a moment this is forever.
Tomorrow, the children will play ping-pong
beneath the trees, the mother's eyes open
to betrayal the father's fist clenched
in disappointment the blood rolling across
the floor wave on wave forever
while the ball spins through shadow & light
to the unchanging cries of bright-eyed children

VOYAGE

She sang and he listened. He knew
after the first few words they were the wrong
words. He didn't put wax in his ears:
this was a modern ship.

Somehow he sailed it into port
with bow smashed and sides raked:
he was one tough captain.
The ship never was the same,

though it sailed pretty well for years. And
when he retired he found the tune followed
him inland. It was too far to heed her call,
but it was his song, after all.

TEACUPS

Life is
Life is impenetrable
"And this, my dear, is the kitchen."
"Forgive me, my dear, I *believe* this is the bedroom."
"Well yes, you may be right . . ."
And trees
trees used to have acorns
but now teacups fall gently from their branches
Yards fill with broken porcelain
"Delightful tea, my dear."
"I'm sorry, *chèrie*, but this is bourbon."
"Ah yes, I should have known . . ."
Children are everywhere
in the kitchen, under the trees
the cries of children overpower our lives
"Mommy! Daddy!"
"Yes children. Yes my dears?"
"Kiss off, old folks.
Rake up those goddam teacups."

HAPPY HOUR

for Frank Dreisbach

Sweet alcohol, god of afternoons,
who carry in the crook of your elbow
the olive and the olive branch, unsheathe
your plastic sword from the flaming stone
and pierce, for us, perception's swinging doors.
En garde, Monsieur Fear, take that
and that. Monsieur Ennui, you rat,
lie down with your mouse, Regret.
Let memory waltz with roses
and Time disappear in the mist;
let the mirrors weep with happiness
at our pagan Eucharist.
O there will be a great consummation,
there will be a righting of wrongs!
If the telephone rings we'll ignore it
while we sing the sad old songs.
We're not afraid of the telephone,
or the dark with its grinning toad;
we're not afraid of the night tonight:
let's have one more for the road.
Common sense should tell us
we pay with pain for our sins
but we won't pay till tomorrow:
today, everyone wins!
Common sense will tell you
drinks and love don't last.
Waiter, here's looking at you.
Lover, fill up the glass.

PORTRAIT: WHITE ON WHITE

Friend, let me list the beautiful number
of beautiful things beautifully white:
mother's milk is white, pillared mansions, soap,
nurses' dresses, their underwear too
(usually), this very page, broken
by this black poem, the stiff veils
of pure brides are snow white, friend, snow
itself is white, our beaches, yes, and daylight,
but the night is dirty and black
like dark water pulling you pulling
you, you yourself are white, by God, and
God is white, baby Jesus and Mary pure
white, friend, pure white, I am sorry
some people are born black as night
black as sin black as deep water that
the decent white people of this world keep falling in

A NECESSARY BUCKET

Klunder, people of sensibility
and moderation are outraged at your lack
of taste. Lying behind bulldozers
is messy and unheroic; it distresses
our practical nation, which sells
vacuums and abhors waste.
Your death proves nothing, the fact
of your bones lying crushed in the April air
only proves what we've said all along:
crackpots and bright-eyed radicals
are always wrong, making the wrong moves
for the wrong reasons. We can't hurry
the seasons: the winter of our discontent
is with us until spring, and so,
if it doesn't break store-front windows,
let freedom ring.

Legislation and debate have proceeded
(at a stately pace) for a hundred years
from the emancipation proclamation
(which wasn't much of a start)
to the present in producing what is needed
to feed the dark beating
of the human heart. While the efficient
silent typewriters recorded the compassionate
words, making no sense at all,
of efficient unsilent Southern senators,
you nestled in the mud like the ground-
hugging plover (making no sense at all),
and got yourself run unromantically over.

Was it suicide, protest, or accident?
Was your heart anguished at
the implacable world, seeing all the lost
children, all the love turned and
twisted, laughter frozen and tears burned?
Or was your own life unhappy,
a failure, did you want it to stop,
did you want to die, lying in the mud
adding your insignificant drop
to the bucket of blood? Ah, Klunder, Klunder,
in this inhuman age, how could you make
such a sad and human blunder?

Was it suicide, protest, or accident?
Does it matter, after all, does it matter
to you, or me? Perhaps it's just this:
so much blood is necessary
to finally tip the scale.
It doesn't matter how we fill
the pail, and you,
Presbyterian minister Bruce Klunder,
lying broken in the mud,
have added your drop to the necessary bucket
of black blood.

PREACHER, SAID THE GENERAL

Preacher, said the General,
are we not able
to carve a cane or a
stick for the glory of God?
Why art thou wroth? and why
is thy countenance fallen?

This rifle now, the M-1
I am offering you, is it not beautifully balanced
(though obsolete)? The curve
of burnished stock
fits snugly the shoulder socket.
Is it not sweet to hear ka-rack
of the spinning bullet, the downward swerve
of adjusted trajectory
zeroing in to the sheeplike target
SMACK at a mile away?
What do you say, is that not
satisfactory?

And tell me, is not
a man-made cloud
a beautiful thing?
(harder than fire and
softer than cumulonimbus,
warmer than summer
and louder than birth and hot
with the holy desire
of man for dominion
over every thing that moveth
upon the earth)

And is this not
our burnt offering
mounting to God?
Are we not Abel
whose smoke rose
from bubbling flesh
to meat-eating heaven,
driving the vegetarian Cain
east of Eden
to the land of Nod?

ELEPHANT TUSKS

The visible world is full of elephant tusks
the music of a silent god
the upward thrust & curve of
natural power, which we grind down
into dice and key, earring and toothpick
to capture the spirit of elephant.
So the spirit of captive elephant
surrounds us; immense shadows
looming from domino and bishop
lean like buildings against our shoulders
until we stagger unaware below this weight.

O the immense weight of elephant
bends our boy's back
as his slender fingers pick at the keys
black & white, through the jungle
of possibilities, the arid plains
of daily practice; the huge stomping
of elephant shakes the floor
until the roof collapses
as discipline fails and our boy crashes
through the wall like Sabu on the back
of an elephant giving
the musical finger
to civilization and its grimy scales

WORLD WITHIN WORLD

I

World within world, like Chinese boxes
the sameness of everything fills one with awe:
rabbits are hunted by people and foxes
and foxes are hunted by dogs with their people
and people are hunted like dogs by the people
who clutch in their foxholes a rabbit's dead paw.

World within world, the shore and the ocean
are made like our bodies of drops and grains
and the earth is a grain in the ocean of sky
and the sky is a drop in the bloodstream of God
and the drops in our bloodstreams are moved by the motion
that moves all the rivers that run in God's brain.

II

And even you, who I think perhaps
hold in your veins the impossible
93rd element, even your eyes
as quick as foxes, the whiteness
of your hand: so many drops
of water; so many grains of sand.

THE DEATH OF THE PILOT WHALES

Every few years, down at the Florida keys,
where bones chew the water like mad dogs
and spit it bubbling out on yellow sand,
the sea darkens, and we crane toward the skies,
toward the airplanes casting their shadows,
but there are no planes and those dark shadows
are not shadows, but mark the silent forms
of pilot whales charging the shore like wild
buffalo charging a train, driving toward
reef and sand till the foam sprays red
below the rainbow stretching from sea to land.

The fierceness of it all, unstoppable,
those broad flukes churning the water, that buried
brain and heart set inflexibly on their last
pulsing, the energy and beauty of all that
flesh turning away from its cold fathomless
world, like the negative of some huge
lemming following God knows whose orders
in a last ordered chaos of frantic obedience
stronger than love. With what joy and
trembling they hunch up the beach,
shred themselves on shoals, what sexual
shudders convulse them at that sweet moment
when they reach—at last!—what
they have burned to meet.

And we, who may be reminded of thoughts
we wish not to think, we tow them back to sea,
cut them open, and they sink.

III
Lines from Key West

I. HERO WORSHIP AT KEY WEST
ON THE 4TH OF JULY

The midget in Sloppy Joe's
had a wooden leg: you said
They don't even make midgets like they used to:
Papa would've used that leg
to stir his drink with.
Drunk, I later slipped on the rocks
and lay on my back in the water
watching the fireworks.
All around there were midgets
watching the fireworks,
their high voices rising like birds
in the darkness. Really, they said, and
Really

II. WRITING THE GREAT AMERICAN
POEM IN KEY WEST

I always believed, he said, the examined life
isn't worth living: all those pores & betrayals,
betrayals & pores. He smoothed the tablecloth;
he looked around. *Mother,* he wrote. *Father.*
And the room became still. The customers cried
in their beer, the bartender cried
saying, You have seen through us,
every one.
     But the tablecloth, that
you'll have to pay for.

III. PLAYING SHUFFLEBOARD, DRUNK, IN KEY WEST, FLA.

So quiet. Even the dogs
were pussyfooting around
under the lights of the shuffleboard court.
Clok went the discs as the critic knocked
the poet out of the "7" box. What
is a breath, the critic asked,
but a weaving of words on the night air's loom?
I don't give a shit, the poet replied.
Don't crowd me.
Give me room.

IV. RESPONDING TO CRITICISM
IN KEY WEST

In Key West, he said,
everyone says "Give it to me Straight."
But he never does because of course everyone
is terribly sensitive and
hurt for years, maybe forever,
by a strong going-over. Still,
this is only natural: hard
to say No, spare me the truth.
Just praise me, for Jesus' sake!
So he finds something positive,
no matter what.

Even this poem, though perhaps
a trifle *prosy*
has its own
je ne sais quoi.

V. LOOKING FOR SOMETHING TO FEAR IN KEY WEST, FLA.

Until now
he had always been afraid of something.
Of the dark, when he was young,
of fists, a little later
and of women, for years and years:
what were they thinking of?
By the time he found out
(he thought he found out)
he didn't care; but still, now
there was something
missing, an emptiness
in his fearbag,
a lack of pain that made him nervous.
Well, I could try sharks, he thought
and jumped in.

VI. TRYING TO HAVE AN AFFAIR
IN KEY WEST

is like looking for young people
in St. Petersburg: you know they're there,
you just have to be on your toes.
The bars float with self-destructive singles
drinking banana daiquiris, the world's greatest
antiaphrodisiac. Everyone
paints in the morning
drinks in the afternoon
confesses everything, everything
by 9 P.M. and passes out
in someone else's house.
Good morning, darling.
Shoot me
quick.

VII. ASHERAH:
SAILING AROUND KEY WEST

for Paul Aziz

The strength of any sloop
is in her stays and
in her name: one
for stability, one
for protection. Ours
was named Asherah,
fairhaired Phoenician goddess
of the sea, a minor deity
and therefore more accessible:
but we weren't sure
until the squall pounced and
the waves curled like jaws
over the foredeck
and the stays held
and we were all speaking
Phoenician.

VIII. WISHING HE HAD A THEORY
IN KEY WEST

He wanted to have a theory, all
great poets have theories, even
though they're nuts (the theories, that is):
Yeats's gyres, Pound's money,
Williams's triads, Olson's
breath, Bly's deep images, and acres of poets
turning Catholic or renouncing Catholicism,
what fun to be so sure of oneself, what fun
recanting one's previous surenesses. And
writing poems about all of this, that
was the point, the poems spill out from
theories, pure peas from piddling pods.

His theory was, to have a theory
you need mainly hunger & meanness
which live on theories
like cannibals on missionaries
but what could he do
in this generous sleepy town
at the end of the world
and him a vegetarian besides?

44

IX. STUDYING POLISH IN ORDER TO ANSWER THE QUESTION WHAT ARE YOU DOING IN KEY WEST?

Studying Polish, he said
is like swimming in spinach
All this rustling, choking
always something stuck
between your teeth
say after me
przymiotnikach
d wadziescia cztery

I knew you couldn't

neither can I

But he keeps trying
because it is the nature of man
to attempt the impossible, dreaming
of the perfect language
the dance whose intricate steps
everyone can follow
some tragic polka
of ninety million broken teeth

X. THE ANGEL OF DEATH HOVERS OVER KEY WEST

From the air, the cerulean water
seemed flat as house paint, a corny postcard:
the Angel casts no shadow so the house
by the baking beach suspected nothing.
It's going good, he said, by far
the best I've done.
A day or so, I've got it licked.
But Jay, she said, you promised that tomorrow
we'd take that little trip along the coast.
Well, maybe, he said. I do need a rest.
The Angel laughed out loud.

XI. THE ANGEL LAUGHED OUT LOUD
IN KEY WEST, FLA.

The Angel laughed out loud.
The Angel laughed
out loud. The Angel
laughed out loud. The
Angel
laughed out
Loud

IV

Trying to Surprise God

THE POET, TRYING TO SURPRISE GOD

The poet, trying to surprise his God
composed new forms from secret harmonies,
tore from his fiery vision galaxies
of unrelated shapes, both even & odd.
But God just smiled, and gave His know-all nod
saying, "There's no surprising One who sees
the acorn, root, and branch of centuries;
I swallow all things up, like Aaron's rod.

So hold this thought beneath your poet-bonnet:
no matter how free-seeming flows your sample
God is by definition the Unsurprised."
"Then I'll return," the poet sighed, "to sonnets
of which this is a rather pale example."

"Is that right?" said God. "I hadn't realized. . . ."

THE HUNTERS: SOUTHEAST AFRICA

Stop! Four men are stalking through the underbrush,
slipping like shadows, shoulders close to ground;
their silent figures deepen the leafgreen hush:
the Headman, the Hunter, the Shaman, and the Clown.
They have killed Time, these dark men who crouch
for weeks beneath the sub-Saharan sun,
whose women dig for roots and weave a couch
of twigs and grass, and cook with stones.

And heart and mind and instinct work as one:
the Headman blazes through their spotted way,
the Hunter kneels, zeroed on their prey,
the Shaman blesses the victim in its blood,
and the Clown will tell the story when they're done:
the rules are clear as those before the Flood.

Look! There are four chambers of the heart
on city street as well as tropic plain,
and four directions from which men can start,
and four dimensions; and four kinds of pain:
tiger pain, maggot pain, elephant, and shark.
Four is the balanced number, the four of spades
lies on the table accusing in the dark:
we have marched on; only our blood has stayed.

And of course we can't go back, back to the bush
or desert, back to the simple places where
soul and body fuse in the antique air.
They weren't really simpler anyway—
and yet . . . something gave us a push
so that we shattered like a pot of clay.

Listen! Deep in the blue North the one wind blows,
to the South a yellow flame flares in their eyes;
like a lantern in the West the red leaf glows
while a green star arcs through Eastern skies.
Listen! I'm trying to be simple: four
men are stalking through the underbrush, they
are in your blood, you are a hunter, or
you are the hunted and they're on their way.

And we lie helpless as a broken wing.
Seeking the secret of wholeness we are lost
in houses we have built at enormous cost;
but tonight I'll howl at the moon, that matriarch
of all divided souls; and I will sing
of tiger pain, maggot pain, elephant, and shark.

THE SNAKE MAGICIAN, NIGERIA

She wasn't very impressive, really.
A large woman, with wobbling naked breasts;
not very young, and not very pretty.

Even the snake hung there in a mealy-
mouthed sort of way, half asleep. At best
one could take them with a kind of pity.

We had come out to see her from the city:
they said she could purify sins. The rest
of the group took one look, cursed, and left,

looking for a place to drink. But I guessed
she wanted to talk. I sat down, warily,
pressed against her in the tiny room. With deft

surprising hands she pulled me to the cleft
of her breasts, and purified me, or nearly.

IN GENTLER TIMES

In gentler times, if times were ever gentle,
you'd blossom in a peasant blouse and dirndl
to linger by a stream below a windmill
while I would weave, upon my poet's spindle,
bright cloth for your white shoulders, a gold mantle
of shining praise to cover love's old temple;
but now, my love, we know no such example
of hopeful days, if hope were ever ample.

Today, hope stutters like a guttering candle,
the dark too dark for love alone to handle;
Godot, because unknown, is worse than Grendel,
and love uncertain seems a certain swindle.

And yet my love, our love's as quick to kindle
as simpler loves, if love were ever simple.

SONNET ON THE DEATH OF THE MAN WHO INVENTED PLASTIC ROSES

The man who invented the plastic rose
is dead. Behold his mark:
his undying flawless blossoms never close
but guard his grave unbending through the dark.
He understood neither beauty nor flowers,
which catch our hearts in nets as soft as sky
and bind us with a thread of fragile hours:
flowers are beautiful because they die.

Beauty without the perishable pulse
is dry and sterile, an abandoned stage
with false forests. But the results
support this man's invention; he knew his age:
a vision of our tearless time discloses
artificial men sniffing plastic roses.

SONNET TO A LATIN PROFESSOR

Marking papers in the veranda, he corrects
declensions while dandy bluejays batter
the allamandas with their aery dissensions;
their knifelike chatter dissects his attention
and life seems less lifelike, more worklike.
He thinks, My life has been recalcitrant
to the vernal impulse and our aviatic friends;
it's time to cross the Rubicon, and make amends.

Yes I'm tired of words, he says
(to himself), and Latin is for the birds.
O let me fly with you to Martinique!
And as if to mock him (tongue-in-beak),
Huius huius huius, decline the birds,
huic huic huic.

CANDLES

In a universe infinitely sub-
dividable, the search for the One
takes on a certain piquancy.
That pile of wax was once a candle stub.
Everything, even air, breaks down, and breaks down:
even light from the sun is pulled down
by gravity, and we (debonaire, burning)
are only particles at a particular frequency.

As we break down and separate
what love, what hate, in part, or whole?
Defiant and afraid, I celebrate
my chain-smoking yogurt-eating soul
and wonder as I go like smoke to skies—
as we grow cold, do we at last wax wise?

MENDEL'S LAWS

I

A monk can do his work on bended knees
inside or out; the bishop looked askance
when Mendel labored in a row of peas
and led the combinations in their dance.
The spark of genius dominates the heavens
and sparkles in the furrow and the loam;
both earth and sky are broken down in sevens
and Christ is captured in a chromosome.

My lover, this was many years ago.
Mendel became abbot and then died.
But all his scorned experiments proved so:
the row of peas spoke truth, the bishop lied.
And what has this to do with us? I'm wild
to know it all since you are now with child.

II

The double helix and the triple star
work in conjunction, like harmonic tones,
and I will praise—how beautiful you are!—
the spiral staircase turning through your bones.
Genetic links, for better and for worse,
bind us to all creation: in my ears
your voice has blended with the universe
and vibrates with the music of the spheres.

Your fingers on the keys at Christmastide,
so effortless in their precise selection,
pick out the ancient chords; while I, beside
you, turn the pages at each soft direction
and wonder at your slender hands because
your fingers follow God's and Mendel's laws.

III

When Eve was cloned from Adam's rib, and stood
by the serpent underneath the Tree
she understood what lovers understood
since first they separated from the sea.
Her choice was meagre; still, she had to choose;
and we, like Eve, have chosen ever since,
face to face, the brown eyes to the blues:
it is the choosing makes the difference.

And in the code that Mendel labored on
our child will be deciphered; there will merge,
in childish shape and spirit, a paragon
where paradox and paradigm converge.
Now I can see Eve's children in your eyes:
completely new, yet linked to paradise.

V

The Laughter of Dead Poets

BIOGRAPHY

I've always said I was a late bloomer.
Took my first steps at 16, toddled
across the street to the bar.
Where ya been, Kid? said the bartender.
I'm a wate bwoomer, I lisped, not mastering
my l's till I was 24.
At 30 I was happiest, a basketball star
in high school (started smoking
at 40, when I graduated).
The next year I began writing poetry,
all those wonderful new words
like "concussion" and "meatball."
I wrote steadily and at 45 published
my first book, called *Juvenalia*,
and became famous, as you know.
I went back to my old neighborhood
to find my roots again, and the bartender said
Jeez Kid
you wuz an early drinker.

MYRTLE THE TURTLE

MYRTLE THE TURTLE   P.S. 222

. because we always said Toity-toid Street and
Shut da daw Miss Endicott devised an exercise
for us so we could lose our accent and become
president of the united states . but Bobby
Pepitone said Shit he din wanna be no president
y'ever see a president chewin gum? nosir . but
we had to do the exercise anyway it was a poem
called Myrtle the Turtle . we were supposed to
recite very clearly There once was a *turtle*
whose *first* name was *Myrtle* swam out to the
Jersey shore but of course we each got up in
front of the class scratching ourselves and
ducking spitballs and said Aah dere once wuz
a toitle whose foist name wuz Moitle while Miss
Endicott tore her hair out . I just visited
Bobby Pepitone and to judge by the way his kids
talk poor Miss Endicott must be completely bald
by now . like a toitle his kids would say .

THE LAUGHTER OF DEAD POETS

Unlisted high in the middle
of the World's Non-Pressing Needs,
poetry towers head and shoulders
below watermelon seeds,
whisky sours, colder beer,
ping-pong balls and little women.

The laughter of dead poets
nevertheless rocks mountains.
Gravely developing a sense
of humus, serious lyricists
cooling in casks like fine wine
polish their bones to the line,
feeding the root that feeds
the tree that slips the leaf that
falls through the air the world needs.

The laughter of dead poets fills this air
as the leaves of their books feather down:
otherwise, gentlemen, would we drown
to no avail of tears.

O to all dead poets grinning bonily
at rocky trees, we should get down
on turkey knees and give thanksgiving.
I herewith give it.
                        (onily,
some of the dead poets
are still living)

GRETA GARBO POEM #41

when I'm with Greta Garbo
she gets very talkative
she likes me to put on my Russian accent
and she plays Ninotchka again
people think we're crazy
especially the waiters at Howard Johnson's
Do you want dessert they ask
Oh no says Greta Garbo
Ve vant to be alone
and she & I laugh and laugh and laugh

TO AN ATHLETE TURNED POET

for J D

Fifteen years ago   and twenty
he'd crouch   line-backer   gang-tackler
steel stomach flexing for
contact   contact   cracking
through man after man   weekend hero
washing the cheers down
with unbought beer

and now his stomach's soft   his books
press out his veins as he walks
and no one looks

but deep in his bone stadium
the roar of the crowd wells
as he shows them again
crossing line after line
with crackling fingers   heart red-dogging
with rage and joy over the broken backs
of words   words   words

3 PACKS A DAY

The first one always makes me dizzy.
The last one I suppose will be the nail
they say it is. If all the mornings,
coughing out of bed, when I have cursed
and said, Never again,
were wrapped around tobacco leaves
and lit, we'd have a smoke to end all
smokes, all right.
                              Well, let's not fight.
We've got along for 30 years; I know
exactly what I owe.
You've carried me through everything
from puppy love to Ph.D. exams.
When chips were down
we always counted on each other. Now,
they're telling tales
about you in the press, that you,
who took me through a thousand inward storms,
are tearing me to bits. Ah, you traitor,
my own true love!
You always gave me fits.

30

for Carol

and are you really 30, little sister?
Your freckles faded, so far ago
back with your dolls all lost & broken
though your dolls weren't much anyway
overdressed mongoloids from Woolworth's & Penney's
whose eyes blinked only with a rap on the head
after which one would stick shut

surely not all is loss when we abandon
the propensity to tears and strident debate
and the pure selfishness of children. . . .
But why am I sad to see you?
Is it because I still owe you $23.75
that you saved in quarters from your allowance
and I spent on my first drinks
usually making me sick?
Remember we were told that alcohol
kills brain cells, as does smoking
and holding your breath under water?
By now I have so many dead cells in my brain
my head's beginning to smell

in shallow water stingrays wait like mines
exploding in the heels of little children
Trout float to the surface of Lake Okeechobee
We must dig in and take our stand
We must stand and fight, little sister.
Turkey Creek, Fort Diablo, Indian Point:
what wonderful names America has!
We need to take them back
buy the old houses, strip off the paint
back to the beam, back to the grain
flowers in the porticoes again
this time not built on someone else's bones . . .

71

I can remember when you were seven
curls and red hair, we could count on each other
You would have crushes on my friends
saving their cigarette ashes in Reynold's Wrap
to keep under your pillow forever & ever
you were a knockout then
you are a knockout still
even at 30

if you're really 30

THE DAY EDWARD FIELD
CAME TO DINNER

The day Edward Field came to dinner
I polished the hell out of the kitchen table
and wore my best casual clothes but no tie.
I thought about sunglasses but decided against them—
he might think I'm afraid to look in his eyes.
Now kids, I said, Dammit, this guy's a poet
and sensitive and a bachelor and I don't want
you to scream or jump on his stomach or play
the piano or sing or anything: just keep out of the way.
And for God's sake, I told my wife, don't ever tell him
I published a poem in the *Ladies' Home Journal.*
We worked on the dinner for three days
and I even chopped wood for the fireplace we never use
and spent hours researching the proper temperature
for red Bordeaux (not knowing he didn't drink).
Waiting for him to come, I sat on my hands for half an hour.
warming them up for the handshake.
Finally, the doorbell rang.
I opened the door, and there he was!

Hello, I said, I hope you like onion soup.

HELEN

A mad sculptor in our park
has fashioned there, in writhing bronze,
the old story of Leda and the swan.
There, the trees are cool and dark
and men may sit and contemplate
the myriad forms that love can take.

And on the cement pedestal, between
the burning figures and the cool grass,
is scrawled in printing recognizably obscene,
Helen Goldberg is a good peece of ass.

Ah, Helen Goldberg, your mortal lover
has proved false, and, what is worse,
illiterate. Tell me, did he hover
swanlike above your trembling skirts
in a burst of light and shadow,
or were you surprised by a shower
of gold, shining like El Dorado
in your surrendering hour?

But probably you shifted your gum from one side
to the other while he had trouble
with his skin-tight pants (not yours)
and you hoped later he'd give you a ride
on his cycle—and anyway love's a bubble
that bursts like gum in feminine jaws.

There should be a moral here, and yet
I'd be willing to bet
there was no swan back then, either,
just a story that brown-haired Leda
made up for her mother to explain
why she was late again,
and her lovely daughter didn't hatch from an egg,
but was born in the same inelegant way
as Helen Goldberg, whose pointed breasts
and bottom-twitching walk
devastated all of 77th Street West,
Troy 23, New York.

DEATH OF A COMPUTER OPERATOR

MY TEETH LONG ERODED
HAIR THIN   LOST AN EYE
LOWER ME INTO THE BOX   MY BOY
I'M READY TO BE DECODED

NO MATTER HOW YOU WORK IT
MAKING TAPES   GIRLS   OR POEMS
THE TRIP FROM GENE TO BONE
IS A SHORT CIRCUIT

THE HISTORY OF HEROES
THE CRIES OF THE SEDUCED
CAN ALL BE REDUCED
TO STRINGS OF ONES AND ZEROES

MY PROGRAMMED INSTRUCTIONS
SHOW THE MOST NOBLE MINDS
THE MOST BEAUTIFUL BEHINDS
ARE ELECTRICAL CONSTRUCTIONS

THE COMPUTER DOES NO HARM
AND ITS GETTING MORE LIKE PEOPLE
ALREADY ITS SIMPLE
TO MAKE ONE THAT FEELS WARM

THE MACHINES METAL POINTS
WILL BE SOFT ENOUGH TO CODDLE
WE'RE WORKING ON A MODEL
WITH HAIR AROUND ITS JOINTS

BUT NOW MY TAPE IS DONE
I WAVE MY RUBBER GLOVE
AND SIGN THIS OFF WITH LOVE
1   0   1   0   1. . . .

MISS ARBUCKLE

Miss Arbuckle taught seventh grade.
She hid her lips against her teeth:
her bottom like the ace of spades
was guarded by the virgin queen.

Miss Arbuckle wore thick-soled shoes,
blue dresses with white polka dots.
She followed and enforced the rules:
what she was paid to teach, she taught.

She said that Wordsworth liked the woods,
that Blake had never seen a tiger,
that Byron was not always good
but died in Greece, a freedom-fighter.

She gave her students rigid tests
and when the school let out in June,
she painted rings around her breasts
and danced by the light of the moon.

THRENODY

for Ruth Clark

The box was brown, the dress blue
the lips bright red. It wasn't you

There were certainly many flowers, though
you never liked cut flowers. We passed
the Golf-O-Rama, yards crammed with junk,
a car with a bleeding deer stuffed in the trunk.
The chauffeur spoke of hunting quail: last
time out he got fourteen. He dressed in red
from head to foot—a lot of nuts, you know,
go hunting these days. He joked and said

This here hearse cost thirteen-five
you're lucky to get out alive

You would have liked that. Your quiet heart
embraced so many people.
The sun broke through clouds at the start
of the procession, then perched on a steeple
near Route 46: that was hard to bear.
But soon skies darkened, twenty-two
cars with lights on went slowly through
mist and traffic, through the oppressive air.

Harlequin trees in black and white
danced your welcome into night

Identical houses, not unlike yours
watched from beyond the hill where you were hid.
Rain sifted down; wind whispered across
the false grass. And though I never did,
I meant to tell you that in truth
you were named right, though now you sleep past caring.
Ah Ruth, Ruth, Ruth, Ruth:
only the compassionate are daring.

RECIPE

Let us say you want to write a poem
yes?
a good poem, maybe not The Second Coming but
your hair is getting thin already and
where's your Dover Beach?

Everything seems somehow out of reach
no?
all of a sudden everyone's walk-
ing faster than you and
you catch yourself sometimes staring not at girls

You live in at least two worlds
yes?
one fuzzy one where you always push
the doors that say pull and
one clear cold one where you live alone

This is the one where your poem is
yes?
no.
It's in the other one
tear your anthologies into small pieces
use them as mulch for your begonias and
begin with your hands

WORDS

for Albert Howard Carter, Jr., 1913-1970

They said/No more words
words are crumbling & peeling away
like old paint
meaning hides behind them
curled in things themselves
in feeling and form
the thisness of the world

You said/Words are living
forms that are always dying
and being reborn
shooting out runners like ferns
they must be planted and
pruned and loved and
what a man says
a man earns

THE ARTIST

He liked best watching TV
Next was shading all the maps
his father threw at him. —*Maybe
you'll learn something despite the tube,
you can color them in*
The felt-tipped pens from the studio:
wet black   the deep blues
orange   yellow   kelly green

At first he followed the lines: France
was purple, Australia blue, all of Russia
a deep brown, not red. But soon the colors spilled
over the lines and over each other: a mess
His father was a successful artist. —*Successful
artists are stronger than their children, otherwise
you kids gobble us up*
white green yellow grey red blue black black black

He'd move through the spectrum warm and cool
darker and darker toward the center:
country   state   city   street   home
Nothing in this world   blacker
than his room. Even his father couldn't find him here
Color is psychological his father said
Pink is the color of laughter
black white green yellow grey red red

When he turned off the TV
he would fall into that little white dot
and pop through the screen
to the nowhere where nobody lived.
Intensity is what he was after.

TO A DAUGHTER
WITH ARTISTIC TALENT

for Deijyan Peri

I know why, getting up in the cold dawn
you paint cold yellow houses
and silver trees. Look at those green birds,
almost real, and that lonely child looking
at those houses and trees.
You paint (the best way) without reasoning,
to see what you feel, and green birds
are what a child sees.

Some gifts are not given: you
are delivered to them,
bound by chains of nerves and genes
stronger than iron or steel, although
unseen. You have painted every day
for as long as I can remember
and will be painting still
when you read this, some cold
and distant December when the child
is old and the trees no longer silver
but black fingers scratching a grey sky.

And you never know why (I was lying
before when I said I knew).
You never know the force that drives you wild
to paint that sky, that bird flying,
and is never satisfied today
but maybe tomorrow
when the sky is a surreal sea
in which you drown . . .

I tell you this with love and pride
and sorrow, my artist child
(while the birds change from green to blue to brown).

82

ADVICE TO MY SON

The trick is, to live your days
as if each one may be your last
(for they go fast, and young men lose their lives
in strange and unimaginable ways)
but at the same time, plan long range
(for they go slow: if you survive
the shattered windshield and the bursting shell
you will arrive
at our approximation here below
of heaven or hell).

To be specific, between the peony and the rose
plant squash and spinach, turnips and tomatoes;
beauty is nectar
and nectar, in a desert, saves—
but the stomach craves stronger sustenance
than the honied vine.
Therefore, marry a pretty girl
after seeing her mother;
speak truth to one man,
work with another;
and always serve bread with your wine.

But, son,
always serve wine.

THE MOUSE YOU FOUND

Yes, the mouse you found
is broken, snapped out of breath
by the copper rib; and yes,
we all break sooner or
sooner in the trap of death,
leaving our bones and skin
as crumbling tokens
to be redistributed
by an old technique
to a darker world
where mice don't squeak.

It's too bad. I maybe
write these words
to make me last longer
or, to give me the benefit
of a doubt, to make *you*
last longer: but it won't work
IT WON'T WORK. You'll find out
that all the mice go down,
white grey or brown. It's hard,
but it's a quirk
of God.

On the other hand,
we do, after all, live forever
till we die
and after that
who wants to live forever?
Not you, my brown-eyed daughter;
not I.

Shirley Kaufman, *The Floor Keeps Turning*
Shirley Kaufman, *From One Life to Another*
Shirley Kaufman, *Gold Country*
Ted Kooser, *Sure Signs: New and Selected Poems*
Abba Kovner, *A Canopy in the Desert: Selected Poems*
Paul-Marie Lapointe, *The Terror of the Snows: Selected Poems*
Larry Levis, *Wrecking Crew*
Jim Lindsey, *In Lieu of Mecca*
Tom Lowenstein, tr., *Eskimo Poems from Canada and Greenland*
Archibald MacLeish, *The Great American Fourth of July Parade*
Peter Meinke, *The Night Train and The Golden Bird*
Peter Meinke, *Trying to Surprise God*
Judith Minty, *In the Presence of Mothers*
James Moore, *The New Body*
Carol Muske, *Camouflage*
Leonard Nathan, *Dear Blood*
Sharon Olds, *Satan Says*
Gregory Pape, *Border Crossings*
Thomas Rabbitt, *Exile*
Ed Roberson, *Etai-Eken*
Ed Roberson, *When Thy King Is A Boy*
Eugene Ruggles, *The Lifeguard in the Snow*
Dennis Scott, *Uncle Time*
Herbert Scott, *Groceries*
Richard Shelton, *The Bus to Veracruz*
Richard Shelton, *Of All the Dirty Words*
Richard Shelton, *You Can't Have Everything*
Gary Soto, *The Elements of San Joaquin*
Gary Soto, *The Tale of Sunlight*
David Steingass, *American Handbook*
Tomas Tranströmer, *Windows & Stones: Selected Poems*
Alberta T. Turner, *Learning to Count*
Alberta T. Turner, *Lid and Spoon*
Chase Twichell, *Northern Spy*
Constance Urdang, *The Lone Woman and Others*
Cary Waterman, *The Salamander Migration and Other Poems*
Bruce Weigl, *A Romance*
David P. Young, *The Names of a Hare in English*
David P. Young, *Sweating Out the Winter*